Elaine DePrince, a former special education teacher, was the mother of eleven – two biological sons and nine adopted children. After losing her three youngest sons with hemophilia to AIDS transmitted by blood products, DePrince wrote *Cry Bloody Murder: A Tale of Tainted Blood* (Random House, 1997), an adult non-fiction/memoir written at the request of the U.S. Senate. *Cry Bloody Murder* had a profound effect on the passage of laws that made blood transfusions safer in our country. She now focuses on young adult memoirs and novels and has written several of them.

Mikey Speaks Out is dedicated to Michael-Noah DePrince, a boy whose courage was responsible for the adoption of six West African war orphans.

Elaine DePrince

MIKEY SPEAKS OUT

AUSTIN MACAULEY PUBLISHERS™

LONDON · CAMBRIDGE · NEW YORK · SHARJAH

Ordering Information
Quantity sales: Special discounts are available on quantity purchases by corporations, associations, and others. For details, contact the publisher at the address below.

Publisher's Cataloging-in-Publication data
DePrince, Elaine
Mikey Speaks Out

ISBN 9798886936490 (Paperback)
ISBN 9798886936513 (ePub e-book)
ISBN 9798886936506 (Audiobook)

Library of Congress Control Number: 2023918625

www.austinmacauley.com/us

First Published 2024
Austin Macauley Publishers LLC
40 Wall Street, 33rd Floor, Suite 3302
New York, NY 10005
USA

mail-usa@austinmacauley.com
+1 (646) 5125767

My gratitude goes to Liam Brown, the Production Coordinator at Austin Macauley Publishers, LLC, who saw the beauty in Mikey's story and chose it for publication. I also appreciate the encouragement I was given by my husband, Charles, who died of Parkinson's disease in 2020 but continued to encourage my writing throughout his many years of illness. I am also grateful to my daughter Mia, who would not allow me to lose heart and give up on my writing, even after the death of her father.

Foreword

This is the true story of a heroic, humorous, and loving boy named Michael-Noah, also known as Mikey. He was my brother, but I never had the opportunity to meet him.

Michael-Noah became a family legend. That is why my mother has told Michael-Noah's story from his point of view in this book. She hoped that learning of the brother I never knew would forever live in my heart, and the hearts of the other siblings who came after him in life.

Though Mikey's story was undeniably tragic, it was also full of the joy of life.

Mia Mabinty DePrince

Chapter 1

Pain and fear… That is what I felt on the day of my birth. I longed for my mother to comfort me. I gazed up at her. I hoped she would look down with tenderness into the inky darkness of my eyes. I wondered if she would gently kiss the pale blonde fuzz on my pink scalp. I wished that she would cuddle me in her arms.

I never heard the sound of my mother's voice. I was born deaf, but she could not have known this in those early moments after my birth. However, it was likely that I would have felt the soft words of a lullaby if she had tried to breathe them warmly on my cheek. But she did not. My mother wanted nothing to do with me…even before she learned about my deafness or my hemophilia A.

My birth mother had intended to give me away, even before she saw that I was not a beautiful baby. I was actually somewhat ugly, disfigured by a cleft lip and palate that left a gaping hole in the middle of my face. My twenty-one-year-old birth mother deliberately kept a physical and emotional distance from me – her firstborn. According to my medical records, she had secretly given birth to me in a motel room. Her own mother assisted her. This grandmother of mine had knowledge of my most pressing problem, the hemophilia A.

This is the name that was given to an ancient disease that caused terrible pain from bleeding into joints and muscles. "Hemophilia A" meant that my blood was missing something that most other people's blood had when they were born. It was missing Factor VIII, a protein that makes blood clot.

Every day, a normal person's veins leak. They usually do not notice when this happens, because veins are located under the skin. Usually only the tiniest, and nearly invisible bruise can be seen. When a vein leaks, the body starts to make a plug, like the kind that is put on a bicycle inner tube. Glue is needed to stick the plug on the inner tube. Glue is made of many different ingredients. If the glue maker forgets to add something to the glue, then it won't be sticky and the patch won't stay on the inner tube.

Factor VIII is part of the body's glue that is needed to patch up the tiny hole in a vein. If someone is born without Factor VIII, then the body glue isn't sticky. In that case, when the vein springs a leak, it just keeps leaking. Somebody with hemophilia A can lose a lot of blood from a leaking vein. If the leaky vein is in a knee joint, the knee can fill up with so much blood that it gets almost as big as a cantaloupe. If the leaky vein is in the head, a person can get so much blood in their brain that the blood might crush the brain. If the leaky vein is in a nose, the person with hemophilia A can fill up a bucket with the blood.

There is only one way for the blood of a person with hemophilia A to stop leaking. That is to add Factor VIII to the blood, so the body can make gluey stuff to stop the leak. However, Factor VIII hasn't always been easy to get. It doesn't come from a plant, like corn oil does. It cannot be mined from the earth like petroleum. It can't be squeezed from the udders of a cow or goat, like milk. When I was born, there was only one place to get this precious Factor VIII, and that was from the blood of another human being.

People gave their blood. Then their blood was separated into two parts: cells (the solid part), and plasma (the liquid part.) The plasma part of the blood got poured into big vats. A company would freeze the vats of plasma, and flakes of different types of protein would drop like snow into the bottom of the vats. One type of protein flake was the Factor VIII. The company who made the Factor VIII would collect the flakes into little bottles. Doctors, nurses, and people themselves with hemophilia A, would infuse the Factor VIII into veins to stop bleeding and pain.

My birth mother might have quietly abandoned me. Perhaps she would have left me wrapped in blankets, and tucked in a basket on the steps of a church. However, my birth grandmother had seen my bruises and bleeding. She knew that these were signs of my hemophilia A. She did not have a hard time recognizing this disease, because my grandfather had been born with this hereditary disease. My birth mother had inherited the ability to pass it on to her children. She did not have the full-blown disease. She was a carrier of hemophilia A, and she passed it on to me.

My grandmother knew that I might die if she did not take me to a hospital in time for treatment. To ignore the hemophilia A would mean risking my young life, so she whisked me away to a hospital in the nearest large city. There were two good things about that. My birth mother came from a small town, where it was common to spread gossip. In the large city, no small-town gossips would spread the news of my unhappy entrance into the world. Also, the hospital had a Hemophilia Center. There my bleeding could be treated, and the risk to my life from cleft-lip and palate surgery would be lessened.

Hemorrhaging was common in kids like me who had hemophilia A. In severe cases, the bleeding was often spontaneous. That meant that it happened without a cause, and mine was the most severe type.

My appearance in the emergency room must have sent shivers down the spines of the medical staff on call. Even the hematologists, specialists in the treatment of my bleeding disorder, had to have been worried by the prospect of getting me safely through the surgeries I would need to repair my face.

Because I soon needed the first of several surgical repairs that surgeons would make to my lip and palate, I spent the earliest months of my life in the hospital. Ordinarily, this would not have been a procedure complicated beyond the ordinary problems associated with facial surgery on an infant. However, cleft palate surgery was a risk in a baby like me, due to the hemorrhaging at the site. It could prevent the cleft palate from closing and healing.

I had less than one percent of Factor VIII, a blood protein needed for clotting. A normal, healthy child had a level of fifty-five to one hundred forty-five percent of this important clotting factor. I needed my Factor VIII level kept close to one hundred percent, in order to get through the surgeries and recoveries. These would require infusions of Factor VIII in my vein two or three times a day.

I wasn't allowed to touch the site of my stitches after surgery, but like all infants, my hands naturally wandered to my mouth. The nurses solved this problem by extending my arms on padded boards to keep them away from my face and mouth. So there I would lie, feeling unloved, in pain, and unable to soothe myself by sucking my thumbs and fingers.

Day after day, mothers and fathers walked in and out of the neonatal intensive care unit, where I would lie alone. I often watched wide-eyed and alert as they lingered over the small bundles in the incubators, or little cribs around me. I would wait eagerly for a parent to stop by my incubator, reach a hand inside and pat me, but to my youthful memory, no one ever did.

Some of the babies sucked at the soft pastel nipples of small bottles, as parents or nurses snuggled with them. I, on the other hand, was fed through a special tube that carried food and medicine through my nose, and into my stomach. To me, mealtime was not a tasty, satisfying source of pleasure.

Limited to a small closed-in space, strapped down, deprived of the simple pleasures of touch, taste, sound, and even the joy of a toy, I found a way to keep myself entertained. With nothing to look at except my extended arms, I discovered that my thumbs made fascinating playthings! With my head turned to the side, I entertained myself by bending my thumbs in odd positions.

On one spring day, I was busy playing with my thumbs when a social worker suddenly plucked me out of my hospital crib. She bundled me in blankets, and carried me off to a new home. My world had suddenly expanded! Or so I thought, as the social worker lugged me outside, with my infant carrier bouncing on her hip. I looked with amazement at the bright sunny world around me! The blustery gray snow days of winter had disappeared.

At first I was fretful, while nestled snuggly under my fluffy blankets. My thumbs had been hidden, and I feared that they were lost to me forever under the layers. However, I soon chortled with delight when I pulled my hands from the blankets and discovered that my thumbs, one on each hand, were still attached.

Eventually, the social worker drove away from the hospital, and pulled up in front of a small house. She unloaded me from the back seat, and carried me to the door of the house. She handed me to a briskly efficient lady. This lady would become my foster mother.

Chapter 2

You might think that life would be better for me with a foster mother, especially one who allegedly had been a practical nurse. After all, the word mother denotes loving care, and who, besides a nurse who was a foster mother, could care for me as well as my fragile body required. However, my new foster mother's false pride in her nursing skills proved to be a disadvantage to me. Though she knew the basic bones about hemophilia, she did not know as much as she needed to in order to give me a normal, happy life.

My new foster mother was under the mistaken belief that any type of activity would cause me to bleed to death. Perhaps a decade or more before, that might have been true, but by the time I was born, Factor VIII concentrate made it possible for many children with hemophilia to lead fairly normal lives. Unknown to my foster parents, I wouldn't bleed and die if my foster siblings played with me, or if I explored the house, crawling, and creeping, like any other baby.

At first, my foster mother dealt with the issue of my safety by keeping me in a padded playpen throughout most of the day. She only handled me to change my diaper or feed me. From this prison, I would watch with longing as my foster father played with my foster brother, a healthy little boy not much older than I was. My foster father would toss my brother about. My brother would giggle uncontrollably while our father tickled him. As I watched them, I would laugh, too. I patiently waited for my turn, but it never came. I had to content myself with the vicarious pleasure stolen from my brother's joy.

Once I started to creep to the sides of the playpen and pull myself up, my foster mother moved me into a large cardboard box. Its flat sides prevented me from grabbing hold of the top rail and standing. What was worse...I couldn't see through that cardboard. Being deaf meant that I couldn't hear what was happening, either. Soon I grew frustrated and angry. I began to throw temper tantrums. I had become my own worst enemy. This behavior led my foster mother to believe that I was severely mentally limited.

At night, my foster mother would put me to bed in the crib. Aha! I thought that finally I had a chance to play once again. Despite the darkness in the room, I would pull myself up and grip the rails. One night, my foster mother caught me doing this. She decided to ask the pediatrician for medicine to take the edge off my energy. It was normal baby energy, but she wanted to curb it, and calm me down. At her request, the doctor ordered liquid Valium for me. Yuck! It tasted like peppermint. What was worst, it dulled and subdued me.

Every morning and every night, my foster mother would slip the bitter Valium into my applesauce. I used to like applesauce, but once my foster mother added the Valium to it, the applesauce tasted terrible. I would fight hard to avoid taking it. I would push it away or spit it out of my mouth.

But these efforts were unsuccessful, just as I was unsuccessful at preventing the foster mother from feeding me in the bizarre way that she did.

Armed with inaccurate information, my foster mother was convinced that a child with a cleft lip and palate, even a repaired one, could not swallow or suck properly. Every meal became an ordeal…a match of wills between us. As I shrieked and struggled to free myself from her grip, she'd force me into a reclining position, and pour liquefied food into my mouth with a spoon. I would choke and gag on it.

Once I began taking my daily doses of Valium, I would feel lightheaded, dizzy, drowsy, and confused. Sometimes my vision would blur. Before medical appointments, my foster mother would give me an extra dose of the Valium, so that I wouldn't struggle during the examination. This became a real problem for me, especially when my intelligence was being tested.

Every time the psychologist evaluated me, my abilities dropped lower and lower. Finally, by the time I was a year and a half old, I was diagnosed as autistic, profoundly mentally retarded, deaf, and legally blind. This was in addition to the severe hemophilia A. It was at this point in my life that my foster parents decided I was so severely impaired that they could no longer care for me.

From the time I was born, the religion-based charity under whose care I had been placed since birth, had been trying to find an adoptive family for me. This agency's effort had been unsuccessful. The likely reason was that the foster mother frightened adoptive candidates with her horror stories about me. So, when my foster parents gave up on me, and the religion-based agency could no longer afford my care. They turned to the New York State Department of Child and Family Services.

The state agency agreed to permanently place me in a nursing home for children in need of critical care. However, an elderly New York State social worker came to my rescue. Just weeks from retirement, she did not agree with the reports about me. She could not contradict the medical reports about my hemophilia, deafness, etcetera, but she did not believe the ones about my mental abilities. She refused to give up on me. She continued to attempt to find me an adoptive home. She was the reason why, on a dark snowy night, a man and woman arrived at the home of my foster parents, requesting to see me.

My life had been a melancholy one. My surroundings had been dim, dreary, dark and depressing. Then, on the snowy night when a man and woman arrived at the door of my foster parent's home, my life brightened. I was surprised to discover that the strangers had come to see *me*! How could that be? Nobody had ever been interested in me, except for doctors, nurses, and social workers, and they mostly pricked, poked and prodded at me. Love and affection had not been a part of my life's experience. Yet on that night, the woman at the door picked me up and cuddled me in her arms!

Chapter 3

It had been very late at night when the strangers arrived to see me. My foster mother was angry that she had to take me from my crib, so she could present me to them. She did not permit the man and woman to stay for long – just long enough to watch as my foster mother took me through my awful feeding ritual, and ranted on and on about all of my problems.

These behaviors had frightened away other prospective parents. I expected no better from the new couple. When the man and woman left, I believed that they would never again return. Yet they appeared at the door the following morning with plans to take me to the mall. My foster mother was angry. She saw that as a problem for her. That day she dressed me in an old, threadbare snowsuit that was inches too short for my long arms and legs. It barely fit me, but it was the only outerwear available for me to wear on that sub-zero day…with the exception of the mittens – those hateful mittens.

The mittens were thick, yellow, and hand-knitted. The fact that they were too large was an advantage, because they covered my exposed wrists. However, they were upsetting to me, because there had been no thumbs knitted onto the mittens. They had been designed to keep me from playing with my thumbs! I howled when my foster mother slipped them onto my hands. I thought that my precious thumbs had disappeared for good.

Before I left on my first adventure ever, my foster mother gave the man and woman my bottle of Valium. She warned then not to skip a dose. The woman slipped it into the glove compartment of the car, while the man strapped me into a car seat. As soon as the car warmed up, and they pulled away from the curb, the woman tugged off my mittens. When my thumbs reappeared, I calmed down and giggled with delight.

The man parked his car in front of a giant box store. I waited with the man in the warmth of the car, while the woman hurried in. She came out with a new stroller, a larger snowsuit, plastic baby bottles, milk, baby oatmeal cereal, and jars of baby food – mostly fruit. Best of all, the woman had purchased fuzzy mittens with thumbs. The thumbs had cute faces stitched on. She immediately slipped them onto my hands, before she loaded everything else into the back of the car.

After he drove away from the first store, the man parked in front of huge building with glass walls. The woman said that it was a mall decorated for Christmas. I had never seen a mall before. It had enormous windows. When we entered, small colorful stores lined the inside of the mall. Christmas trees, decorated with bright lights and glittering ornaments, blinked cheerfully. I was so thrilled by the mall that I didn't know whether to stare at the Christmas trees in awe, or play excitedly with my thumbs.

While we were there, the man and woman stopped at a toy store. They bought a bag full of toys, including different colored boats and ducks. I was filled with joy when they gave me the toys. No one had ever bought me such fun gifts. The only toy I had ever owned was an inexpensive homemade stuffed fabric snowman.

After shopping, the man and woman found a restaurant in the mall. It was filled with wonderful smells. They sat down in big chairs, and propped me in a smaller chair that hooked onto the table. I watched intently while the woman opened the package that contained plastic baby bottles. She retrieved a tiny pair of scissors from her purse, and cut an "x" into the tip of one of the nipples.

Then she ordered apple juice. A server washed out the bottle, and the woman filled the bottle with the juice. I never drank out of a bottle before. My foster mother had insisted that I was unable to suck on a nipple, so she had never allowed me to use a baby bottle. Now the woman wrapped my hands around the bottle, and helped me hold it to my lips.

I guzzled the juice down as the woman fed me one baby food jar of macaroni and cheese, and another of chicken and vegetables. Finally, the woman gave me a large, round object to chew. I didn't know that this hard object was a cookie, because I had never chewed on one before. It was sweet and yummy.

After my belly was stuffed full of food, the man and woman drove me to a motor inn. There, the man filled the bathtub with warm, bubbly water. He then added the colorful boats and ducks to the water. The woman stripped off my clothes, and placed me gently into the tub. I began to splash in the water, and float the boats and ducks all around me. I played for such a long time that I forgot my thumbs. When the woman dried me off with a fluffy towel, I discovered that my thumbs and fingers were wrinkled. I was pleased to see that the wrinkles eventually smoothed out.

While the woman was dressing me, the man poured a teaspoon of Valium down the drain to hide the fact that he had not given it to me. Then he heated a cup of milk in the microwave, and mixed baby oatmeal in the bottle with the milk. I drank all of it on the way to my foster parents' home. When I finished, the woman hid the bottle. By the time we arrived, I had fallen sound asleep. My day had been so exciting that I hadn't needed the dose of Valium. I was so sleepy that I didn't even see the man and woman leave.

When I awoke the following morning, I was disappointed not to find the man and woman there, waiting for me. I thought for sure they would still be standing in the living room, where I had left them. I wondered where they had gone. I began to cry when I didn't see them, but my tears stopped, and I smiled when they suddenly showed up at the front door.

On that morning, my foster mother gave them my bottle of Valium, and all of my other possessions. I didn't own much, only a small, worn backpack of hand-me-down clothing, a blanket, a box of disposable diapers, and my stuffed snowman. I was glad to see that the snowman was coming with me. I was very attached to it, but then it was my only toy with the exception of my new bath toys. The woman's face fell at the sight of so few possessions, and she was clearly disappointed that though I had hearing aids, they were too small to be useful to me.

Again, the man and woman took me for a ride in their car. This time they did not go to the mall with all the lights, though I hoped that they would. Instead, they headed to the hospital. As soon as I saw this, I began to cry. When we arrived, I curled up and snuggled tightly in the woman's arms. I was relieved that the woman did not turn me over to the doctors or nurses to get an infusion of Factor VIII injected into the vein of my arm.

The man took a package that the nurse gave him. With me still clinging tightly to her neck, the woman examined the contents. I peeked from between my fingers and saw that it contained several boxes of Factor VIII, butterfly needles, syringes, alcohol wipes and small cotton sponges. I began to shiver with fear, but I never did get that infusion of Factor VIII on that day. It was for emergency purposes. I eventually learned that much more Factor VIII would come my way, but not just now. With the box in tow, the man and woman left the hospital with me.

I wondered where we were going, as the man drove the car onto the highway, and headed southeast. Eventually the sky grew dark. That was when I realized that it was too late to return me to the home of my foster parents. Oddly enough, I was not saddened by that thought. My life had not been a happy one with them. I hoped that perhaps it might be happier with this new set of parents. I was so excited by the thought of a new home and new parents that I remained wide-awake for hour after hour. As we drove, I watched the lights of all the cars and trucks whizzing by in the blizzard that surrounded us. In the wake of the tractor-trailers that passed on our left, snow would fly up and blanket the windows of the car. This wonderful sight took my breath away. I'd become so distracted by the flying snow that I would forget to play with my thumbs on the way home.

I was still wide-awake in the glitter of the snow and the glow of the full moon when we arrived at my new home. Two older boys, who lived in the house, rushed out to greet me, in their thick fuzzy, footed pajamas and flannel robes. On the trip, I had already concluded that the man and woman were my new parents. Now I realized that the large excited boys were my big brothers. Without hearing aids, I could not figure out what their names were, but I would eventually learn that they were Adam and Erik.

The outside of the house was brightly trimmed with merry lights. Two large, cheerful snowmen stood on the front lawn. Inside the house a twinkling Christmas tree blinked at me. While my mother rocked me in a large antique chair, I drank a bottle of warm milk. After the long ride home, I finally fell asleep in my mother's arms. Unknown to me, my new father carried me upstairs to my bedroom. In the middle of the night, I woke up in a cozy crib. I was covered with a soft comforter. My old stuffed snowman was tucked in my arms. A little light with a clown in floppy shoes that carried red, blue, and yellow balloons, stood glowing on a nearby bureau. It was the first time that I could remember sleeping in a lit room.

How I had hated the dark bedroom in my foster parents' home. Being deaf deprived me of one of my senses. Sleeping in the dark had deprived me of another. I had always been frightened by the dark. The light in my new bedroom gave me a warm happy feeling. Soon I fell sound asleep again, comforted by the funny little clown with big shoes.

Chapter 4

I awoke the next morning to a totally different life. I looked out the window at the snow that was still falling. I wondered what highs and lows my new life might bring me.

That morning, no one restrained me, reclined me, or caused me to gag by spooning mushy food down my throat. Instead, my mother sat me in a high chair, and scattered Cheerios on the tray. She dropped slices of banana on the tray too, while she poured milk over bowls of cereal with sliced bananas for the big boys' breakfasts.

I watched with amazement as my brothers first ate, and then scurried to gather coats and backpacks. I gazed through the windows as they ran outside to meet the big yellow school bus that pulled up in front of our home. They were going to school, and I wanted to go with them. I cried when they left.

After my big brothers had climbed onto the school bus, Mommy turned to me. I had not eaten a single Cheerio, or taken one bite of banana. Instead, I sat with my arms out to my sides, reluctant to touch anything. I was expecting my mommy to feed me as I had been fed in my foster home. But she didn't do that. Instead she cut the bananas into even smaller pieces. She mixed them into a yellow bowl of Cheerios, and poured yogurt over everything, so it would all cling together. Then my mother held my fingers gently around the handle of the spoon, and she patiently helped me scoop the mixture into my mouth. After a few minutes, I managed to figure out how to chew and swallow the solid food. I could tell from the smile on my mother's face that she was pleased by my effort.

After I was full of food, my mommy bathed me in the tub with the boats and ducks she had bought for me in Buffalo, New York. Then she dried me and dressed me in flannel lined corduroy overalls, appliqued with a spotted puppy. I also wore a yellow and white long-sleeved shirt, socks, and red shoes. Finally, my mother slid me into my new warm snowsuit.

Uh-oh! I must be going to the doctor's office, I thought. I began to cry and throw myself around, fighting with all my might to tear off the snowsuit. My new mother struggled to calm me down, and get me into the car.

When my mommy backed the car out of our driveway, and headed down the street, I remembered that I was in a new home. I couldn't tell where we were going, but I knew when we arrived that it wasn't the hospital. We stopped in front of a large building that resembled a hospital, but it was different in many ways. People in wheelchairs, assisted by nurses, didn't line the entry. Instead a long line of shiny metal carts stood waiting by the door.

One by one, people grabbed a cart as they entered the building. Some would pop their small children into a seat at the front of the cart. This is what my mommy did when the doors sprang open, and led into a huge room with shelves full of food.

This building was a supermarket, and I had never been to supermarket before. As a matter of fact, I had never been to any food store before. In this store, there was so much food, and so many choices! In one aisle, my mommy picked up jar after jar of baby food. Each one had a label with a picture of the food that was inside. Mommy showed each of them to me before putting them into her cart. I bounced with excitement as I examined them one by one. Some jars were filled with fruit: apples, pears, peaches and plums. Others were filled with vegetables: corn, peas, green peas, string beans and sweet potatoes. Some of the jars were filled with meats, even little hotdogs.

In another aisle, my mother found some boxes of large round cookies, like the ones she had given to me in the restaurant. This time, Mommy opened a box and gave me a cookie to chew on. Even though I couldn't hear myself, I was so pleased by the cookie that I hummed as I chewed it.

Last of all, we shopped in the juice aisle. It was filled with an array of fruit juices in all flavors and colors: purple for grape juice, red for cranberry juice, brown for prune juice, orange for orange juice – of course. At first I frowned at the apple juice bottles. The juice inside was the color of pee-pee. Mommy opened one of the little bottles and coaxed me to taste the juice. Yummy, it was sweet and tasty, like the juice I drank in the restaurant. I knew then that it couldn't be pee-pee.

I decided that the most boring aisles were the ones that sold fresh meats. At home, I turned my nose up at that type of food. Mommy did too, but Daddy and my brothers loved pork, beef and chicken…the foods that were sold in the fresh meat aisles. I preferred the meat in the jars. It would be a long time before I was willing to accept meat, and then I only liked hamburgers.

Every day, I watched from the large front window of the living room as my father drove off in his small blue car. Soon after Daddy left for work, my brothers would once again climb up the steps onto their yellow school bus. My mother was the exception. She didn't go to school, nor did she go to work away from home at that time in my life. Instead, she worked from home, typing stories to send to magazines, and short funny stories with pictures of animals to keep me entertained.

Mommy also spent time taking me on outings to different places. Though I soon became used to the comings and goings of Daddy and my brothers, I always expected mommy to be by my side… my constant companion and a continuous part of my daily life, the person who was opening the whole world to me.

Eventually, my mother introduced me to hamburgers. When we arrived home after shopping or going to lunch, Mommy read me stories, and later we would each take a nap. In the late afternoons I would wake up to the vibration of feet pounding across the floor, and up the stairs. Then I'd pull myself up to a standing position in my crib, eager to peer out my bedroom door, and watch my brothers enter to lift me out of the crib, and play with me.

Chapter 5

One morning, two days before Christmas, Mommy baked a fragrant batch of crispy almond cookies. She packed the cookies in a tin, and dressed me, once again, in my favorite blue corduroy overalls, with the sweet spotted puppy on the front. Then she bundled me into my snowsuit, and together we headed out to a Christmas cookie swap at a friend's home. There, other mothers carried in the tins of cookies that they had also baked. Like my mommy, those mothers opened their tins of cookies, and set them around the dining room table to be admired and sampled by everyone.

One moment I was sitting contentedly in my stroller, munching on a cookie Mommy had given me. Suddenly my mother disappeared from my view. She had left me alone with all those strange mommies. Was she gone for good? Would she return to me? I cried, sobbing until I began to hiccough. Then I spied her, hurrying toward me with a cup of milk and a second cookie. My mother put the snacks down on the tray of my stroller, and then picked me up.

She hugged me and kissed me all over my crumb-covered thumbs and tear-smudged face. I laughed through my tears, feeling happy that Mommy hadn't lost or forgotten me after all.

That day, I felt something that I hadn't experienced before. Never had I cared for someone like I cared for my new mommy. It was the first time that I had felt love. Though my momentary loss of my mother had been painful and frightening, her return filled me with great joy.

Soon I began to notice a pattern within my family. Mommy played with me during the day. My brothers played with me in the afternoon after school. Daddy played with me after dinner, and at bedtime. At night, it was Daddy's turn to sit with me in the large wooden rocking chair, and read books to me. As Daddy read, he pointed to the black squiggly shapes on each page. Soon I began to love this fun Daddy too.

Nearly every day Mommy bought me new things that would enrich and brighten my life. They weren't always toys or books. Once she bought me a special hearing aid with two cords. Each cord had a little plug that went into each one of my ears. On another day, Mommy bought me a padded leather helmet that would protect my head if I fell. My mother taped the hearing aid onto the top of the helmet. This helped me hear some of the words that Daddy read to me. I didn't hear the words clearly and well, only faintly, but even that little bit made the words sound fascinating to me.

On another day, Mommy took me to an eye doctor. Within days, I had a pair of glasses that changed the blurry world I had grown used to, into a crisp, clear world. With the glasses, I was finally able to see well the shapes of the black smudges in the picture books that Daddy read to me. Even though I still found it difficult to hear what my father was reading to me, I quickly began to understand the concept that each movement of Daddy's mouth was linked to the squiggly shapes in the books. Soon I realized that each group of shapes formed a word. I began to read these words! No one knew this, except me…but soon they would.

One day, Daddy brought a black box home from work, and hooked it up to the television set. Suddenly, letters that I recognized from my picture books, popped up on the screen. Much to my surprise I realized that the television was reading to me! Now, when no one else was free to read to me, I could turn on the television, and it would read to me. As in real life, the movement of the characters' mouths were linked to the words on the screen. This made it easier for me to understand what was being said.

I had turned two-years-old shortly after that first Christmas in my new home. I received a pile of toys, blocks, and a bright red and yellow wooden riding horse. I received small cars and trucks that I could scoot across the floor, and large toys with handles that I could push. If only I could walk them across the room.

I had grown frustrated by my inability to walk. Every day, my mother would hold my hands, and help me to walk across the kitchen or living room. My legs, which were weakened by the inactivity in my foster home, couldn't hold me up. I was fine as long as I cruised or crawled from one piece of furniture to another, but I wanted to walk and run across the floors like my brothers.

On one snowy morning in February, the doctor sent my mother and me to visit a small shop in Philadelphia. There, a man measured my weak legs with measuring sticks and tape measures. When we left the shop empty-handed, I was disappointed. I wondered what that was all about. Why would someone be interested in the size of my legs?

Two weeks later, we returned to the shop for a surprise. This time, the man presented me with a pair of metal braces. They reminded me of the legs that the robot, C-3PO, wore in the *Star Wars* film. Though Mommy referred to them as short leg braces, I was certain that they were C-3PO legs, and I was thrilled to get them.

The man clipped the braces into the sides of a pair of new shoes, and wrapped a thick leather strap around the calves of my skinny legs in order to hold the braces in place. Once the braces were on my legs, I was able to walk across the room alone…without holding Mommy's hand. Within moments I was running. Mommy had to chase me around the shop to catch me, while I giggled with mischievous glee.

When we arrived home that afternoon, Mommy tried to take my C-3PO braces off my legs in order to tuck me into my crib for a nap, but I refused to part with them. After a short struggle, Mom gave up, and I fell asleep, happy with my braces. When I awoke, I banged the braces against the crib rails, laughing at the sound that reverberated. It was so loud that even I could hear it.

That afternoon before the yellow school bus arrived home, I hid in the kitchen under the table. The moment my big brothers opened the front door, I ran gleefully toward them, and threw myself into their arms. They tossed me into the air, and when they put me down, I followed them everywhere, chasing them from room to room. Then they would suddenly turn and chase me back.

I was overjoyed by the fun we were having together. I felt just like them, a regular boy. Maybe I even felt better than them because I had C-3PO legs like a Star Wars character. I suppose I had not yet developed self-consciousness at that young age, so it never occurred to me to wonder what the rest of the world thought of a little boy like me. I was covered in bruises from my hemophilia. I wore a hearing aid taped to the top of my helmet. I also wore a pair of red eyeglasses, and ran around with C-3PO legs.

Chapter 6

It was my C-3PO legs that caused me to end up in the
hospital for the first time after moving into my new home. I
had been running around in the family room one afternoon
and *BAM!* I ran right into the television. I knocked it off the
TV table and it fell over on top of me. It left me with a
swelling on my chest, shoulder and underarm.

Mom packed us each a suitcase of clothing, and drove
us to the hospital. When we got there, I was admitted to
pediatrics, the children's ward. The nurse placed me into a
large crib. I was very scared. I was sure that Mommy would
leave me in the hospital alone. I started to cry.

The doctor gave me Factor VIII, but he left the tube in
my arm. I held on tightly to my mother, sobbing the entire
time. Then I sat on her lap, while she rocked me gently.
Suddenly a man pushed a cot into my room. The nurse made
it up into a bed for my mom. That's when I realized that my
mother was going to spend the night with me.

Before bedtime, Mommy and I ate dinner in our room.
Later we had ice cream for a snack, while we watched
television. Before I fell asleep, I was given more Factor
VIII, but it didn't hurt because it went right into the tube.

I stayed in the hospital for two more days. While we
were there, the doctor taught Mommy how to give me the

Factor VIII at home. Soon it was time for us to go home. I never had to go to the hospital for an infusion of Factor VIII ever again. My mother gave it to me at home forever after.

The following year, when I was three years old, my parents enrolled me for half-day classes in a Communication Handicapped preschool class at the local public school. I was supposed to be learning Signed English there, but because of my poor motor skills, I had difficulty speaking with my fingers. However, unbeknown to my teachers, I had an uncanny skill for reading lips and reading. Though I couldn't speak, I was able to understand everything that was being said around me.

Early in the afternoons, when I returned home from school before my brothers, I would sprawl out on the family room floor and read the newspaper. I'd mumble loudly the sounds, as I *read*. I'd watch the lips of my mommy's friends and laugh, when they'd say, "How cute! Michael-Noah is pretending to read." Little did they know that I was really reading.

At that stage in my young life, my reading was so good that the teachers at the preschool I attended began to question the extent of my hearing loss. The Child Study Team wanted to place me in a program for children with very low intelligence. My mother disagreed with this decision. She believed that I was very smart, otherwise how could I be reading? Whenever she mentioned my reading, members of the child study team scoffed. They just didn't believe her. They continued to insist that I was a very slow learner.

Mommy was convinced that my primary problem was deafness. Consequently, she arranged for me to have my hearing tested several times in different medical centers.

These results varied from time to time. Sometimes the tests proved that I had perfect hearing. At other times, they proved that I was totally deaf. That was because I thought of each test as a game, and enjoyed the attention these evaluations were bringing me. My parents and the Child Study Team were frustrated by these differing results. Only one member of the team sided with my parents' opinion of my abilities.

Finally, after many tests, my mom came to a very clever conclusion. She believed that as long as I faced the audiologist during the test, I would do very well in my hearing evaluation. However, Mommy had a difficult time convincing the audiologists that the excellent result was due to reading lips, and following visual cues. She finally convinced one audiologist to test my hearing with my back to him. That audiologist agreed to try this, and that time I failed miserably, proving my mother's point. Other audiologists were still not as easy to convince of this. As a result, I was bounced around from one testing center to another.

When I was five years old, I finally experienced my first success in a school program. Once more this was a program for the Communication Handicapped, but the new teacher caught on quickly that I was unique. She recognized that I was able to read lips, read books, and follow verbal directions. She also realized that my math skills were excellent for my age.

For the next two years, I loved attending this school. The teachers were kind, considerate, and treated me very well. Though the other children were not on my academic level, they were friendly, and the teacher depended on me to help them with their schoolwork. The only disadvantage to this school was its distance from home. Little did I know at that time what a disastrous effect this distance would have on my future, but I didn't worry about it then. I was having too much fun to think about things like that.

The following two years were ideal out of school as well as in school. My family loved to take camping trips, and I did too. I enjoyed traveling to different places, and seeing fascinating scenes and animals. I believed that family vacations were the best and most adventurous part of my life, but I was a mischievous child, and often got into trouble during those trips.

On one particular vacation to the Gaspé Peninsula in Quebec, Canada, I was feeling especially rebellious. I was five years old at that time. In the morning, after our first night on the Gaspé, I flushed my hearing aids down the toilet of the cabin where my family was staying. My Dad had to dig them out with a wire coat hanger. I had a very patient father. He didn't get angry. He just laughed.

Two days later, on an island in the middle of the Gulf of St. Lawrence, I threw my eyeglasses over a cliff. Adam caught them as they soared through the air. Otherwise they would have landed among the nests of the gannets in a wild bird preserve. It was Daddy who reached out a hand and grabbed my padded leather helmet, as it followed the glasses over the cliff.

My hearing aids didn't do much for my poor hearing, so I didn't miss them, but I really did need the glasses and the helmet. Without the glasses I couldn't read. That was something I loved to do. Also, we were going on a whale watch during that vacation, and I would not have been able to see the whales without my glasses. As for the helmet…without it I could have been severely injured if I had fallen and bumped my head.

That trip to Canada was the last one on which I caused so much mischief. It was also the last time I was left behind with my mother at the campsites, while my father, Adam and Erik climbed the mountains. On that trip they had taken a hiking tour to the summit of Mont Albert, a tall flat-topped mountain in the Chic-Choc range of the Gaspésie National Park. I was resentful about missing the excitement; however, I was soon distracted when a black bear and her cubs wandered through our campsite, tempted by the berries that grew around them, and attracted by the scent of the fish that my mom had baked on the grille.

By the end of that summer, I had developed some degree of common sense about the outdoors. I no longer thought it was so funny to toss my possessions into the surf or over the cliffs. I began to take hiking very seriously. Thanks to my C-3PO leg braces, which my parents attached to hiking boots, I became a sturdy and proficient hiker.

In the final week of the summer, my family hiked to the huts at Lonesome Lake on Cannon Mountain in the White Mountains of New Hampshire. By dinnertime on the first day, everyone reached the huts by the lake, but the climb had been steep and difficult. That night the entire family sat by the lake to watch the Aurora Borealis, the Northern

Lights, which glowed in many colors throughout the dark sky.

It took a second day to reach the summit of Cannon Mountain. Some of the paths were vertical hikes that required wooden ladders, pegged into the cliffs, in order to climb straight up the mountain.

The older boys and Daddy reached the summit first. Mom and I were pokier. We were caught in a storm of sharp ice. It slowed us down, and forced us to take shelter in the trunk of a fallen tree that seemed as large as a cave. We were so drenched by then that we changed into heavier clothes and raingear.

Because of the bitter cold on the mountain, the family expected to return to the base by the Arial Tramway. However, it had taken Mom and me so long to reach the summit that the tram was ready to abandon us before we got there. That meant we would be stranded on the mountaintop through the dark, cold night. Dad had to beg and plead with the operators to wait for Mom and me.

When Adam and Erik saw us coming, they rushed to us. They took our packs. Their concern and caring effort made it easier for Mom and me to run the last five minutes so we could reach the tram in time. We barely made it before the tram headed down the mountain.

Chapter 7

My family life changed in more ways than one after that exciting summer, when we hiked in the mountains. Because of a knee joint bleed, I became the first to learn how it would change.

That autumn my dad began to travel around the country on business trips. My mom began to do volunteer work. She served on a committee that acted as a link between adoptive parents of special needs children, and the State of New Jersey. Quite often my mother left the house after everyone went off to school. One morning in early winter, when she had an important meeting to attend at the State Capital in Trenton, I awoke with a knee joint bleed. As a result of my bleed, I could not go to school that day.

That morning, the bleed wasn't caused by an injury. It was a spontaneous bleed, which meant that it was caused by nothing at all. Still, my mom couldn't send me to school with the bleed. She gave me Factor VIII, bandaged the knee, bundled me up against the cold day, and took me with her.

I must admit I enjoyed going with her. While Mom attended the meeting, I played with toys that were stacked in the corner of the director's office. I also watched everyone's lips carefully to eavesdrop on what they were saying. The meeting was about a family who had adopted a child with problems. I didn't think that meeting was interesting, but it soon turned to a different topic. I perked up when the director told my mother that there were two little boys in New Jersey who had hemophilia A. They were living in a hospital, and they needed a family to adopt them.

The director asked my mother if she and my dad would be willing to adopt them. Mom saw me staring at their lips intently. She turned to me and said, "Well, Michael-Noah, you have two big brothers. Would you like two little brothers as well?" That would mean I would have four brothers! I would be the middle brother instead of the youngest. I'm sure that my face glowed brightly with the idea.

That afternoon, as we were leaving the Trenton office, I thought that Mom and I would pick up the little boys from the hospital, and bring them home to be with us right away. I was disappointed when I saw my mother say to the man, "I'll need to ask Charles first. If he agrees, then we'll take them. I'll have an answer for you immediately after Christmas."

Immediately after Christmas! How many days away was Christmas? I remembered that I had come to my family shortly before Christmas a few years before. Why couldn't the new brothers come before Christmas, too? I convinced myself that they would, but Christmas day came and went. The little brothers did not arrive. Maybe my little brothers would arrive for my birthday, I told myself. My birthday fell on December 27, but still no little brothers came through our front door.

Around this time, a new disease was spreading through the hemophilia community. It was the HIV virus. It caused a disease called AIDS, and because it was transmitted through blood products, and Factor VIII was a blood product, Mom and Dad wondered if AIDS would become a threat to me, and to my new little brothers. Unknown to me, my parents had learned that the new brothers had tested positive for HIV. Mom and Dad decided it would be wise to discuss the adoption with my hematologist.

The hematologist told my parents that an HIV positive test result meant that only the virus had passed through my new brothers' systems, and they had developed antibodies to it. The antibodies would make them immune to the actual disease of AIDS. The hematologist truly believed what she was telling Mommy. Because my mother trusted every word the hematologist said to her, my parents decided to go through with the adoption. That made me very happy.

After Christmas, we did not take our tree and decorations down. We wanted them there for my new little brothers. A few days after my birthday, a car pulled up in front of our home, and two tiny boys, stepped out. They were named Teddy and Cubby.

The boys were with their social worker, and I watched her complain, "The hospital sent them home last night instead of keeping them in the hospital. They had not even lasted one day before the older one was back in the hospital with a head injury. We were there for four hours waiting for him to get Factor VIII!"

By this time I was old enough to know that head injuries required not one, but several infusions of Factor VIII. From watching my mother's lips as she explained this to the social worker, I learned that the infusions had to be given at least eight hours or twelve hours apart. The social worker looked surprised when my mother asked, "Where's his Factor VIII supply?" The social worker answered, "I don't have any."

I gasped with shock at her answer. Even I knew that she should have brought Factor VIII with her. Mom and Dad carried it wherever I went. Suppose the social worker had crashed her car on the way down the New Jersey Turnpike to our home?

I watched as my mother telephoned the hospital where the boys had been treated for their hemophilia. I saw her explain to the nurse that she had a cabinet full of my Factor VIII, and that I was on homecare. Homecare meant that my mom infused my vein with Factor VIII whenever I needed it. The nurse said that she would send Factor VIII for the new boys, but my mom could use my Factor VIII until the new shipment was delivered.

That afternoon, I watched in wonder while my mom gave Teddy my Factor VIII…just like she had been giving it to me for years. Factor VIII became a very important part of the lives of the two youngest boys, just like it was a part of mine. Soon the boys started to go to my hematologist and my doctor had Mommy give factor VIII to them every two days, like she gave it to me. After that Teddy and Cubby rarely had spontaneous bleeds. They were now able to do nearly everything that other boys did: play ball, ride bikes, swim, and hike mountains.

I loved having these new brothers. We played together every day. Even though Teddy and Cubby would argue with each other, they never argued with me. Teddy was very smart. He and I loved to read together. Mom and Dad were always taking us to the bookstore to buy books. Cubby was too young to read on his own. Adam would often read to him. As a family, we had wonderful experiences and began storing up great memories. We believed, that as the years passed, many more good times would follow.

Chapter 8

In the summer of 1986, Mom and Dad thought it would be a good idea to make Cape Breton Island in Nova Scotia, Canada, the destination of our trip. We had been talking about adopting a puppy from the dog shelter. Mom warned us that if we did, then we could no longer go to Canada. So we decided that this would be a good year for a final trip to Canada. We would adopt the puppy as soon as we returned home.

Before we went, Daddy insisted that we get into shape for Nova Scotia by spending a week hiking in the mountains of the Shenandoah National Park. Everyone but Mom got into shape on that trip. She had the bad luck of stepping into a hole in the ground, and breaking her leg. She would need to be in a cast for eight weeks!

Immediately after our camping trip to Virginia, and before we left for our trip to Nova Scotia, Teddy, Cubby and I went to New York City with Mom to see the hematologist. We were late getting there because Mom was slow-moving in her cast. When we finally arrived, a Midwestern television news reporter was waiting with the doctor in her office. The reporter wanted to interview my mother and the hematologist about AIDS. This was the same hematologist that had once told my mom that the three youngest boys in the family would not contract AIDS from HIV.

As a result of what the doctor had told my mother, Mom said to the reporter, "As a mother of sons with hemophilia, my greatest fear is that my children will be hit by a car. They stand a greater chance of dying in an accident than from AIDS."

After that, my mother went off to have her pink and green striped cast removed, our family headed off on our camping trip to Nova Scotia. On our way up we stopped at the Bay of Fundy in New Brunswick, Canada. Dad told us that the Bay of Fundy had the highest tides in the world. We were eager to see them.

While we were at the Bay of Fundy, we walked out onto the muddy beach. Along the sides of the beach were high cliffs. The watermark on the cliffs showed that the high tide was about twenty feet up! We had to walk down a long stairway to get to the beach. Once we were there, Teddy and I helped Cubby dig in the mud for stones. We brought them back to the campground. We were covered with mud. We definitely needed a bath. Dad filled a small kiddie pool with water, but it was too cold. Mom boiled a bucket of water on the campfire, and we added the warm water. Then we washed all the mud off of us. We washed the stones in the leftover water.

Digging for stones in the Bay of Fundy was great fun, but not as much fun as hiking to John D. Lake in the wilderness of Northern Nova Scotia. The hike was seven miles each way, and we camped in tents at the end of the trail.

That morning, when we started to hike, the weather was nice, but Dad had forgotten to listen to the radio for the weather forecast. While we were at John D. Lake, Hurricane David blew in and knocked our tents down during the night.

In the morning, Mom had to give us our Factor VIII before we could walk the seven miles back to our campground. First we needed to get one of our tents standing, so that Mom could mix our Factor VIII and infuse it in our veins. While she was doing that, Adam shouted, "Hey! There are moose walking around out here."

Mom acted very brave while she gave us our Factor VIII. Later, when we got back to our campsite, she admitted that she was scared. "Suppose the moose walked all over the bottles of Factor VIII?" she said, but they didn't, so there was no harm done.

On that hike we ran into a mama bear and her cubs. We saw plenty of moose. A great horned owl landed on our pop-up camper, and the beach got washed away in the storm. But none of our supplies were damaged, especially not the Factor VIII, which we had stored in a metal cooler chest.

In September, when we returned from Canada, I didn't have a care in the world, except how much money I had saved from my allowance. I wanted to use that money to buy a new World Globe, a wall map of Africa, and a computer program about Africa. I had always been in love with the continent of Africa. I had learned the names and capitals of every country there. When one of the countries changed its name, I learned the new name. But neither my old frayed map, nor my old globe had the new names on them, so I was excited about getting the updated maps and globe.

I also loved the children of Africa…those starving big-bellied children of Mozambique, and so many other war zones. I had always dreamed of helping them, but other than donating my remaining allowance funds, which were rather puny, I didn't know how else I could help.

Except for my deep concern about the starving and sick children of Africa, life was great for me that year. My speech had developed despite my cleft lip and palate, and my deafness. That Christmas, after our Canadian vacation, had been the greatest so far. There had been lots of snow, so my four brothers and I spent a lot of time sledding on the hills near our home, and ice-skating at our favorite lake. Then on a bitterly cold morning in early February, everything changed for the worst.

My school bus was running late that morning. Mom was giving Cubby his factor VIII for a very bad nosebleed that wouldn't stop, when my bus finally pulled up in front of our house. Knowing that my mother was sopping up Cubby's blood, I didn't wait for her to help me get settled on the bus. Instead, I hurried out the door, and hopped aboard the bus on my own. I reached for my seat belt, but I couldn't find it. I tried to tell my bus driver to help me, but he wasn't listening to me. Instead he was paying attention to his own daughter. She had missed her own school bus that morning. He didn't want her to be late for her pre-school.

As soon as I climbed aboard the bus, the driver speeded away from the curb, in a hurry to get to his daughter's pre-school. Once the bus driver dropped his daughter off at her school, he hurried onto the highway in the direction of my school. He was going way too fast, and another car tried to pass him.

My school bus, which was really a Chevrolet Suburban, did not have a good rollover rating. Even though I was into cars, trucks and other motor vehicles, I was unaware of that unsafe fact. I was shocked when suddenly the driver swerved, and the Suburban rolled over.

Because I was not wearing my seat belt, I was thrown from the Suburban. An ambulance was called to the scene of the accident, where I was found wandering in the highway close to oncoming cars. The ambulance took me to the trauma center where a hemophilia center was located.

I suffered a severe skull fracture, which tore the protective covering of my brain. I required brain surgery, because hundreds of bone splinters needed to be removed from my brain. The fracture was located in the speech center of my brain; I lost all of my speech. This was devastating to me because I had worked hard on speech therapy for many years!

As a result of the head injury, I also developed a disease called diabetes insipidus, which damaged the pituitary gland in my brain. The diabetes insipidus resulted in an imbalance of fluids in my body. This imbalance caused me to produce large amounts of urine. It also made me very thirsty, even if I had plenty to drink. I was left partially paralyzed, and my eyes were damaged by my head injury.

Despite the grave tragedy of the school bus accident, the worst was yet to come. In May of 1988, Mommy brought Teddy, Cubby, and me to the hematologist for our yearly hemophilia check-up. Cubby had a fever that day. It wasn't a high fever, but it was a sign of terrible news for all three of us.

Chapter 9

On the day at the doctor's office when Cubby had a fever, Teddy, Cubby and I were tested for HIV. Though we were not told this at the time, we all tested positive. Only Mommy was told this bad news, and she only shared the secret with Daddy. We kids wouldn't learn the bad news until later.

This would not have come as such a big shock to my parents, if our hematologist had been correct about her opinion of HIV and AIDS. Instead of us just catching the virus, as she had predicted, Teddy, Cubby and I all contracted the full-blown disease of AIDS from our infection with HIV.

That evening when we returned from the hematology clinic, Mom and Dad carried a huge box of maps into the kitchen. We boys were all very excited to see them. To us maps meant a trip. We wanted to know where we would be going, but our parents made us wait until after dinner before telling us what the maps were all about.

After dinner, we all pitched in to clear the table and load up the dishwasher. Then we crowded around the kitchen table to watch our parents spread the maps around. There were dozens of maps from places all across the United States. We just could not wait to find out where they were going to take us.

We were shocked when Mom and Dad told us that we could choose anywhere we wanted to travel for our family's summer vacation this year. We would go anyplace we wanted to go, and we could see anything we wanted to see. It would be a one-month dream vacation, and we couldn't believe our good fortune.

We circled the table, and intended to take our turns by age, but Dad refused to tell us his choice. He wanted to keep it a secret, so Mom got to choose first. Her choice was the Great Salt Lake in Utah. Adam was second, because he was the oldest child. He had always loved Northern Wyoming, so he chose Grand Teton National Park. Erik came next. He loved to draw dinosaurs, so he chose Dinosaur National Monument on the border of Colorado and Utah.

Since I was the middle boy, I made the next choice. It did not surprise anyone that I chose Africa. My brothers laughed at me. "Africa's on a different continent. It's too far away!" they said. My parents were nicer about my choice of Africa. They explained that the family could not afford a trip to Africa at that time. If I went, I would have to go alone by plane. I gave this some thought. I decided to wait a few more years, especially since there were many wars and diseases in Africa. Instead of Africa, I made a second choice: Yellowstone National Park. I had read that it was a huge place full of wildlife that I had never seen before, as well as bubbling lava, giant geysers, and hot springs.

Teddy, who was reading the complete Laura Ingalls Wilder's series of the *LITTLE HOUSE* books that summer, wanted to cross the prairies of the mid-west and find a buffalo chip. I laughed at him. I couldn't imagine carrying bison poop home in a bag. Cubby chose Mount Rushmore

National Memorial because he was a great fan of Abraham Lincoln, one of the four presidents who looked down from the side of the mountain.

Once I accepted that Africa was not an option, I had a wonderful time traveling west with my family and our new dog, Stripe. On this trip, we panned for gold, and viewed dinosaur fossils and caves. We saw bison up close, as well as elk, pronghorn antelopes, mule deer, coyotes, and wolves. We saw eagles flying off steep cliffs. We swam in the Great Salt Lake, which looked like and felt like it was filled with cooked spinach. Teddy even brought home a buffalo chip, but none of us wanted to sit next to it in the van.

That summer of 1988 was the hottest summer of the twentieth century…a real record breaker. Our van's air conditioning failed on the second day of the trip in Saint Louis, Missouri. We tried to get it repaired, but the repair only lasted one day. It seemed to get hotter and hotter as we drove west. Mom and Dad joked about how it was the exact opposite of their trip to frozen Niagara Falls years before, when they had traveled in the blizzard to get me. On this summer trip, the weather was over one hundred degrees for sixteen straight days!

I had some scary adventures on the summer trip. One of them took place in Mammoth Cave National Park. Nobody had chosen it, but we thought it would be fun to visit anyway as we passed through Kentucky, early on in our trip. These caves were really huge with beautiful mineral deposits inside them. The caves are deep in a mountain, and lit with electric lights. The tour guide wanted to show us what the caves looked like when they were first discovered.

To do this he needed to turn off all of the lights, but he only gave us about a two second warning. This was not enough time for Mom and Dad to warn me about the dark.

When the guide flicked off the lights, not only could I not hear, but also I couldn't see. Suddenly I was in a pitch-black world. I started to scream. I felt like I was going to lose my balance and fall off the steps. I grabbed Daddy's legs tightly. Dad became frantic. He was trying to hold me up, and at the same time trying not to fall over the stairs and into a crevasse below. I managed to cling to Dad like sticky tape. When the lights came back on, he had to peel me off. As scary as all this was, if was still an exciting adventure…perhaps even a once in a lifetime adventure.

Oddly enough, in the midst of the drought, our most frightening adventure involved rain. We were camped in Rio Blanco State Park, located somewhere around the Colorado-Utah border. We had arrived in the campground after dark. There were no lights, no rangers, and no other campers. It was totally dark.

Dad said, "This is an arroyo. If it rains, it will fill with water. Suppose it floods?" We all decided that there couldn't possibly be a rainstorm in the drought. However, Daddy kept our pop-up camper hooked up for safety. He made us pack everything we didn't need in the van. Adam and Erik would sleep in their tent, the one that didn't need pegs. It could fold down instantly. Dad insisted that if it rained, we needed to get out of there in a few minutes flat – no messing around!

Last of all, we all walked to the bathrooms with flashlights. Inside the bathroom there were cliff swallow nests all over the walls. The floors were littered with broken eggshells. Swallows were flying in and out. Daddy took turns picking up Teddy, Cubby and me, so that we could peek into a nest. We found little tweeting birds inside.

After we used the bathroom, we shined our flashlights into the bushes and trees surrounding our pop-up. Lights glowed back out at us. Suddenly, mule deer walked onto the campsite. It had been their eyes that had glowed at us. Finally, the two older boys crawled into the tent. We three younger boys climbed into the pop-up camper with Mom and Dad. Enough excitement for the night! We fell sound asleep in what seemed the middle of nowhere.

CRASH! BOOM! Early in the morning, before the sun rose, a crash of thunder and flashes of lightning woke us from our deep sleep. Mom jumped up and started to grab us. She threw us into the van. Stripe jumped in with us. I could feel the thunder, and I was too shocked by the lightning to even figure out what was going on.

Adam and Erik quickly folded and stuffed their tent into the back of the van. They helped Daddy close the pop-up. Just as the rain began to pour down in enormous sized drops we pulled away. We hurried to get out of the sand-bogged campground as quickly as possible.

We headed off to Dinosaur National Monument. It was fascinating to watch the paleontologists dig out fossils from the cliff walls. We camped there, and in the late afternoon of the next day, we did a bit of camping up a small mountain. Suddenly the sky grew dark, and we headed down the mountain. Cubby started to cry on the way down. He seemed to be very scared, but I didn't know why because I couldn't hear what was going on.

I was feeling proud because I had been very brave when we got to the bottom of the mountain. I hadn't cried – not once. When we got back to our campsite, I learned why Cubby had been crying. Everyone had heard a cougar, but me!

Daddy had chosen a special place to visit. He kept it a secret until we arrived there. It was someplace that I had never heard of before. At first when Dad pointed to the sign, I thought it was going to be a fiery place because it was called Flaming Gorge. It was located on the Green River in Wyoming, not very far from the dinosaurs we had visited. Despite the drought that the whole country was experiencing, Flaming Gorge was not on fire. It was called Flaming Gorge because the cliffs were all shades of red and orange. They reflected off the water like fire. It was stunning to see as we drove toward it, and even more beautiful to watch as we took a pontoon boat through the flickering water of the gorge.

Our parents gave us each a turn driving the pontoon boat. That is except our Golden Retriever, Stripe. He didn't have hands to steer the boat…just paws, so he sprawled on the deck admiring the view, and watching the sheep and antelope hop all over the slopes. I had to admit that Dad had made an exciting choice. I would never have known it existed, if not for him.

After Flaming Gorge, we headed to the Great Salt Lake in Utah, where the water was warm, salty and filled with what looked like cooked spinach. Because of its saltiness, it was a very buoyant place to swim. There we met a couple from Alaska! The woman was Inuit (Eskimo). The warmth of the lake fascinated her. She explained how all the water in Alaska was cold, so she enjoyed this lake, and we all had a great time swimming with her.

As we traveled further north through Wyoming, we encountered forest fires. Wolves and coyotes had panicked in the Grand Tetons during the fire there, causing them to run through our campsite, howling into the night. We all stood frightened, and stiff as trees as they rushed by. Though they were only within an arm's length of us, they were too frightened by the distant smoke and flames to bother us.

The very next day, we decided to drive out of the Grand Tetons and into Yellowstone National Park. The fire had worsened and just as we reached the entrance, Park Rangers stopped us. They wanted us to turn back immediately, but Mom burst into tears and told them, "We've traveled all the way from New Jersey for the trip of a lifetime. We might never be able to make this trip again."

We were very lucky that Mom did such a good job of crying so pathetically. The ranger felt sorry for her, so he let us in. We were the last family allowed to enter, and the last family able to get a camping spot in a fenced-in area where we would be safe from bears and cougars.

We spent two days in Yellowstone. During that time we watched the volcanic activity of the paint pots and the spray of geysers into the sky. We would have liked to stay longer but the fire suddenly went from little sputters creeping along the ground, into enormous flames and that leaped high into the sky. Soon everyone was chased out of Yellowstone by the rangers. Firefighters had arrived because the fire was out of control.

Considering that he was a dog, we hadn't given Stripe a choice of vacation site, but he found a place that he loved anyway. He was a furry dog, and all the heat overwhelmed him that summer. It didn't surprise me that he loved our next stop.

Toward the end of our vacation, we crossed onto the Upper Peninsula of Michigan and settled into a cool and refreshing campground along Lake Superior. It was an amazing place because there the temperature dropped from one hundred degrees down to sixty-five degrees. It was too chilly to swim in the lake, but we didn't care. We did enough swimming in the Great Salt Lake. In Michigan, we enjoyed the canoeing. While we all shivered and wore heavy sweatshirts, Stripe wasn't bothered at all by the chill. He swam so far out that we worried he might cross all one hundred and sixty miles of the lake's width.

At that campground on the lake. we met another family with five boys. They camped next to us. They were all about our ages, and they worked with us to build enormous castles in the sand. They didn't have a dog to help them, but Stripe was willing to help all of us with the digging. With ten boys sharing a campsite, we had a happy ending to our vacation.

Chapter 10

As August came to an end, our family drove home to start school. This new school year of 1988 did not begin well for Cubby and me. Cubby was sick all the time, and I got kicked out of the state school for the deaf. I was expelled because one of my classmates wore shoes covered with glitter. Well, to be honest, that wasn't exactly the reason why I was asked to leave. I suppose I could say that was a *contributing factor*. My high reading level was the real reason.

Though I was nine years old, my reading was on level with the high school students at the school. Once more, this made my teachers suspicious of my ability to hear. However, I must admit that my classmate's shoes did play a significant role in what happened that fateful day.

When my teacher noticed the girl's glittery shoes, she commented on them to another teacher. I read the teacher's lips, then looked down at the shoes and laughed. Before I knew what was happening to me, my teacher gripped my arm and marched me down to the principal's office to have my hearing tested for at least the fiftieth time.

When the audiologist tested me, he did not face me away from him. Instead, he insisted that I face him. This gave me the opportunity to watch the audiologist closely. Every twitch of the man's shoulders or arms gave me the clear signal that he was clicking on a sound. I responded to the movement by putting a small ball into a bucket to prove that I had heard the sound. The truth was that I hadn't heard it at all. I had used visual cues. By this stage of my life I had become a perfectionist, so I faked the results of the test. I did a good enough job of pretending to hear, that I earned a perfect score on the test, just as I had done once before as a small child.

The principal telephoned my mother, and asked Mom to come get me. Within an hour, my belongings were packed up, and I was on my way home. I hadn't realized that by faking my test results, I would be asked to leave the school for the deaf. Now where would I attend school?

Fortunately, soon after I left the school for the deaf, I was scheduled to have a CT scan of my brain to check up on the damage done by the accident. The doctor had a clever idea. He decided to test my hearing while I was under anesthesia for the scan. He explained to my parents that this hearing test would be more accurate than the one I had been given at the school, because I would be unable to fake the results.

Sure enough, the doctor was correct. Not only did the audiogram show that I was totally deaf, but the CT scan showed the reason why. I had been born without inner ears! Sound could not travel from my brain to my ears! This meant that my excellent reading skills were due to my intelligence, not my hearing.

Now the Child Study Team in my town didn't know what to do with me. They came up with all kinds of ideas for my education, some excellent, but others quite terrible. The psychologist on the team wanted to put me in a class for cognitively impaired children – children who were once referred to as mentally retarded. "Why?" my mother wanted to know.

"He looks like he would fit in well there. He looks slow and he has poor coordination," the psychologist insisted.

The social worker argued, "What does that matter? He has a high I.Q.!"

High I.Q.… low I.Q.… deaf or hearing… My mom realized that the argument between the two would go on and on, unless she came up with a better solution – one that would not only meet my needs as a deaf student, but a student with serious medical problems as well. Mom suggested that I should be home schooled, and the Child Study Team, sick and tired of the arguments, carried this out.

Home schooling might have worked well, if the teachers they had chosen were more imaginative. However, they were stuck in the mud of their beliefs that my disabilities limited my intelligence.

My teacher brought easy reading books – ones for primary grades. She started with first grade level books. I complained that such easy books bored me and insulted me. These books led to many arguments between my teacher and me. One day, after one of our arguments about the books, the teacher allowed me to choose a book that I liked. I loved Science Fiction, so I chose the novel *E.T. (The Extra Terrestrial)* by William Kotzwinkle. My teacher laughed and told me that I would never be able to read that book. However, she was willing to let me try.

The teacher assigned me a certain number of pages for homework that week. On the last day of the week, she tested me on what I had read. I had seen the movie *E.T.* and had immediately noticed that there were differences between the book and the film. One of the major differences had to do with the candy that Elliot used to bribe ET to follow him home.

On the test the teacher had asked, "What candy did Elliot use to bribe E.T. to follow him?"

I wrote, "M&Ms."

My teacher marked the answer with an ugly red 'X'. She claimed that the answer was Reese's Pieces. Being deaf, I couldn't gauge the volume of my voice, when I shouted, *"WRONG!"* But it must have been very, very loud and furious. It had caused my mother to run into the dining room from the kitchen where she was preparing lunch. She found that both the teacher and I were red-faced with anger.

Mom tried to settle the argument. She asked where I had gotten the idea that Elliot used M&Ms. I opened the book to page forty and stabbed word M&Ms with my finger. The teacher's jaw dropped, and she sheepishly admitted that she had not read the chapter.

By the end of that school year, I was reading more difficult science fiction. This led to another argument with the same teacher when I chose to read *Contact* by Carl Sagan. It was nearly a four hundred-page book, and I read it in one night, leaving the pages scarred by my thumbnails. My teacher didn't believe that I had read it, until she watched me read Ray Bradbury's *Fahrenheit 451* in less than one hour. When my mother and teacher both saw me flip the pages of this book with my thumbs, they realized how I had left the identical scars on the pages of *Contact.* I was a speed-reader! I amazed both my mother and my teacher with my total comprehension, and complete recall of everything I read.

The following year, I was assigned to a different teacher. Cubby and I shared this teacher. Her name was Bernice. She was like a grandmother, and we both loved her. Bernice was kind, and she had a great sense of humor. She understood my quirks, so she and I never got into arguments. Cubby worked with Bernice in the mornings. I worked with her in the afternoons.

During the time Bernice taught us, she became my mother's best friend. Every day, Cubby would order take-out lunch. He and I would then enjoy our lunches with Bernice and Mommy. Joanie, the young woman that my mother had hired to help her take care of us, soon joined us for lunch too.

Every afternoon, Cubby took a nap, and Bernice worked with me on my schoolwork. I used to play all kinds of tricks on Bernice. It was easy to do because she was not very good at computers. I loved geometry but I hated Algebra II. Every afternoon, I would program my computer to fail when I typed in Algebra II. This made it impossible for Bernice to teach me that subject. After much frustration, she would move on to other subjects. My favorite of which were the sciences, especially the biological sciences that I studied from medical textbooks that my mother bought from a medical textbook store.

My parents owned thousands of books. By the time I reached my teen years, I had read just about every book on their shelves. That is when I started to insist on reading the medical books. They were complicated, so at least I couldn't whiz through them by speed-reading. My favorite texts were in neurology: the study of the brain, and hematology: the study of the blood. Bernice found them to be difficult reading, so she left me on my own with them. Instead she worked with me on Chemistry, Physics, History, Geography and Political Science. I loved politics. Bernice and I liked to follow it on television with closed captioning.

It might have seemed like I had grown up to become a serious boy, but I didn't. I continued to display my sense of humor. For example, every Christmas holiday, I would search my parents' closet for my Christmas gifts. Every single year I would be caught because of my sneakiness. One of my parents or older brothers would find me tiptoeing out of my parents' bedroom with a bag of gifts in my arms. I never understood why I was caught doing this. Because I was deaf, it never occurred to me that paper bags made crinkling sounds.

I also borrowed my older brothers' computers to play games. When they were in school, I would sneak into their rooms, and hook up all of the computer games we owned. Cubby and I would set them up in my bedroom, and there we would happily play until it was time for high school to let out. We liked it when they had after school activities. It gave us more time to play with the computers.

Stripe always warned us when my older brothers crossed the road between their school and our house. That was when I'd fill Cubby's wagon with computers, and sneak them back into my brothers' bedrooms.

Eventually, Teddy, Cubby and I learned that there was a reason we were sick so often. The tests we had been given by the hematologist in the summer, proved that we had

AIDS. As we grew sicker and sicker, we began to realize that this disease was fatal. We were not going to get well!

You might think that this part of our lives would be very sad, but our family and friends filled our lives with fun and laughter. My two oldest brothers enriched my life, and the lives of my two youngest brothers. Adam, who was five years older than me, was a computer genius. He would always win First Place in New Jersey Scholastic computer competitions. I was little more than a toddler when he first taught me to use computer applications. As I grew older, he taught me to actually program the computers. It was to Adam that I owed my knowledge of changing my mathematics programs to frustrate my teacher. He would sit down with me at my computer and work for hours on developing my computer skills.

Adam also taught me to ride a bicycle. However, after my school bus accident, I could no longer balance on my two-wheeled bicycle. I remember sneaking outside and trying to ride my new blue bike. My parents had given it to me for my birthday six weeks before my accident. I longed to ride it, but was never able to do so after that fateful February day.

It was to my brother, Erik, that I owed my other great interest. Erik loved art. He spent many hours at the kitchen table teaching Teddy, Cubby and me how to draw. He focused on science fiction drawings. My favorites were the detailed images he did of Star Wars craft, especially the Millennium Falcon. After he would draw me a perfect picture of the Millennium Falcon, I would bring it to my mother's office, and copy dozens of images on her copier. Then I would sit down with a pair of sharp scissors and cut

out the images. I would use the cutouts to make up stories
of my own. Eventually, I had collected hundreds of images
of different spacecraft. I stored them in a cigar box, and
carried them wherever I went. I played with them like toys.
They became my favorites.

Chapter 11

On Cubby's tenth birthday, I had a weird experience with bigotry, and it had nothing at all to do with AIDS. Because it was Cubby's special day, we took our new recreational vehicle out for a trip. We let my youngest brother choose the place where he wanted to celebrate his birthday. Since we were already in the White Mountains of New Hampshire, he chose the Alpine Slide in Bartlett, New Hampshire. Dad bought each of us all-day tickets for the Alpine Slide. We knew the ride would be wild, so that morning, Mom gave all of us Factor VIII to protect us from a bad bleed.

All of the boys in our family were experienced Alpine sliders, but some kids in the line were not. In front of the slide there was a giant sign that said, "DO NOT STOP ON TRACK." This was a very important rule, because the Alpine Slide curved and curled around the track. There were many large bushes and trees along the track. They prevented someone coming down in a sled from seeing more than a couple of feet in front of themselves. If the rider in front of them stopped on the tracks, there might be a collision.

Certain of these rules, we lined up for our rides on the slide. My brothers and I were having a crazy time that day. Hundreds of kids kept going down the slide at super speed.

At the end of the ride, they'd jump up and get in line again for the ski lift to take them back up to the top.

Sometimes people, especially kids, weren't too careful on the slide. They didn't brake at the bottom. Then they would hit the sled in front of them before that rider had a chance to get up and out. This happened to me once, and I was thrown from the sled. I got scratched up, but I had my Factor VIII flowing in my veins, so I didn't care. I just jumped up and ran back in line again for the ski lift.

Life was just grand for me on that sunny summer day, until the moment of the second accident. A girl who was about nine years old caused this accident. She seemed to be scared of riding the slide. She came down the slide creeping like a snail. At the bottom of the slide there was a steep section that you could hit as you came out of a blind curve. The girl chose that spot to stop dead on the tracks. I had the bad luck to stop immediately behind her. My sled hit hers. She wasn't hurt, and she wasn't thrown out of her sled, like I had been. She just got scared and began to cry.

The girl had a big loud father who started screaming and yelling. I couldn't hear him, but I sure could see him yelling. He said that I gave his daughter a whiplash. Dozens of little kids had been accidentally knocked out of their sleds that day. Everyone knew that this was a risky activity. They expected to get bumped around a little. No one blamed anyone else, except this one father. He insisted that the accident happened because I was handicapped. He said the operators of the ride should not have allowed me to ride the Alpine Slide.

The father of the girl complained to the manager of the Alpine Slide, and the manager called the police. When the police arrived, they put our family in the back room of a dark closed-down restaurant. They began to question my family. The police wanted all kinds of information about my handicap status. They wanted my parents' identification and mine as well.

My mom and dad were upset by this treatment. They insisted that I did nothing wrong. Besides, what twelve-year-old boy carried identification? My parents also tried to explain that the girl was wrong because she did not obey the sign. She had stopped on the tracks.

I felt that I was being picked on because of my disability. My brothers and I were getting scared. We were worried that the police were going to arrest my parents and me. If the police took me from my parents, who would care for me, and my hemophilia?

I looked out the window, and noticed that the girl wasn't hurt at all. She was outside playing, laughing, and running around with her brothers. Yet the police weren't letting us go until Mom and Dad agreed to give them my name and address…which they would not.

Suddenly the police officer that was questioning us left the room to make a telephone call. He asked other police officers to come in for back up, and take us into the police station. Dad said to Mom, "This is just too freaky. Obviously this policeman never read the constitution. Go out the back door with the kids. I'll go out the front door and sidetrack the policeman. I'll meet you down the road somewhere."

Dad grabbed his backpack and walked out. He wanted to be seen so as to distract the police attention from me. He was successful. The policeman saw Dad, and he started to follow him, while the rest of us headed out the back door. To do this, Mom, Adam, and Erik had to climb over old tables and chairs that blocked the back door. Adam and Erik lifted Cubby, Teddy and me over the furniture. Then we all snuck out to the camper.

As soon as we reached the camper, Mom told us to get onto the floor and hide. She changed her shirt from a lady's flowered shirt to a man's striped one. Then she put a man's hat on her head and tucked her long red hair inside of the hat.

By this time, somebody had noticed that we were gone. The people who worked at the Alpine Slide were searching the parking lot for us. Mom pulled out of the parking lot and drove down the road. After we pulled away, Adam and Erik looked out the window and saw the Alpine Slide employees peeking inside all the other cars and campers.

Mom drove into the next town, and she parked in a lot behind a tractor-trailer. We waited about a half hour. Cubby, Teddy and I were hiding on the back bed, covered with a blanket. Because Cubby and Teddy were dark skinned, and I had a cleft lip and palate, Mom was afraid the police would recognize us.

I worried about Dad. Mom drove back toward the Alpine Slide, while Adam and Erik looked along the side of the road for Dad. I wondered if he had been arrested when we escaped. Mom told me that he would be safe. He had been wearing a yellow Mickey Mouse shirt and hat, but he would change into the light gray plaid shirt, and a gray golf hat that he had in his backpack. Suddenly Erik shouted, "It's Dad!"

As we drove by, Dad stuck his thumb up as though he were a hitchhiker. Mom stopped the RV while Adam helped Dad hop in. Then we drove away…far away from the Alpine Slide.

When I look back on that day, I realize that we were experiencing prejudice. Me for my disabilities, and Teddy and Cubby because they were dark skinned in an area full of light skinned people.

Chapter 12

The year we celebrated Cubby's birthday at the Alpine Slide was the year I had won the lawsuit against the school bus company that caused my accident. Before that year, my family could not afford to camp in fancy recreational vehicles, so we camped in tents and pop-up campers throughout my childhood. It was my accident, and my resulting health problems that led me to spend the money I had won in my lawsuit to improve my life, and the lives of my brothers.

In the spring before our trip to New Hampshire, my parents explained the lawsuit to me. They sat me sat down at the computer and told me that I had a lawsuit filed in Court against the company that caused my bus accident. They said I would soon be settling the lawsuit for this accident. They believed I had suffered so much in the accident, that the money I would win in the settlement of my case should be spent on items that I wanted and needed.

My parents asked me, "Is there anything special that you want, Mikey? Make a list, and we will fill your requests." The lawyers for the bus company thought that I had no understanding of what this settlement would mean to my family and me. They were mistaken. My list included items that would especially benefit my brothers and me. On the computer screen I typed: an indoor in-ground pool, and a recreational vehicle.

The one we bought first was the RV, which we used on Cubby's tenth birthday, when we drove to the Alpine Slide in New Hampshire. The RV was easy to buy, and the reasons we bought it were just as easy to explain. The recreational vehicle might have seemed like a foolish request to those who did not have a clear understanding of how AIDS and hemophilia was affecting us. However, for years, when my brothers and I were well, my family had camped in pop-up tents. Sometimes these pop-ups were overheated in summer afternoons, or freezing in fall evenings when temperatures dropped. Once we were sick, we could not deal with these changes in temperature.

I realized that a recreational vehicle would protect the family members with AIDS from inclement weather while we were on vacations. It would also provide a place where the family could safely carry medical supplies, or use electricity to run intravenous pumps when sleeping, or traveling on the road. As our AIDS progressed, Teddy, Cubby and I often needed pumps to treat pneumonias. We also required intravenous antibiotics or gamma globulin to boost our immune systems. The RV allowed us to receive these treatments while crossing the country or sitting on a mountaintop in perfect safety and contentment. It also enabled us to drive the long, hard ninety miles to and from the Children's Hospital AIDS Program, while sleeping comfortably in beds.

My father traveled regularly for business, thus the physical wellbeing of my younger brothers and me fell on the shoulders of my mother. Mom would regularly load us into the family's van at six in the morning for the trip to the clinic. The wait at the clinic often stretched on for many hours, while Mom waited for Teddy, Cubby and me to receive care. On one occasion, we spent ten hours at the clinic. On the return trip, when my mom nearly fell asleep on the busy turnpike, I insisted on purchasing the RV. It provided my mother with a place to pull over, and rest along the busy turnpike.

The RV provided another advantage to my family and me. Early on in our disease the county newspaper had published an article about the incidence of AIDS in children. In the article, the newspaper revealed the fact that there were three little boys in our county who had AIDS. The neighbors, knowing that the three youngest sons in our family had hemophilia A, jumped to the conclusion that we were the afflicted children. Unfortunately, this conclusion was accurate. Consequently, Teddy, Cubby and I were ostracized. Only one boy in the entire neighborhood wanted to play with us.

Adam and Erik, who neither had hemophilia A nor HIV, would have been lumped into that category with us, if it were not for the fact that the newspaper had mentioned three sons, not five. Nonetheless, as members of the same family unit, they often fell under suspicion of having it. Therefore, my RV benefitted everyone in the family. No one we met on our vacations knew that we had AIDS. Our lengthy annual family vacations in the RV protected all of us from the bigots in our neighborhood.

At home, my family soon learned that there were many more bigots in our neighborhood than we realized. These bigots crept out like evil monsters during the building of the pool. If I thought the incident at the Alpine Slide was one of bigotry and hatred, what came from the building of the pool was far worse! And we needed this pool badly.

My parents used to take us to swim in lakes. Then one summer, despite being immunized for all childhood diseases, I contracted measles. Measles could be deadly to a child with AIDS. My mother, who had grown up in the days before the Measles, Mumps and Rubella (MMR) vaccine, clearly remembered what they looked like, and the experience of contracting them. As soon as she saw the itchy red speckles that covered my body, she contacted the infectious disease specialist who treated me at a pediatric AIDS program.

Most of the specialists there were too young to have witnessed measles in their patients. "Can you bring Michael to me, so I can see his measles? I've never seen them before," one young physician told my mother. Consequently, my mother drove me the long distance to the hospital. Sure enough, I had measles, but it wouldn't be long before many other pediatric AIDS patients with weakened immune systems would catch measles, too. It seemed that despite vaccines, kids with AIDS did not have the ability to develop the antibodies needed to protect them from measles.

Following my bout with measles, I was no longer allowed to swim in public places. This was a devastating blow to me, because I loved swimming nearly as much as I loved reading. The pool was a way to lighten this blow for all three of the boys in our family with AIDS.

Once Adam and Erik were of driving age, they could jump into the family car, and head off to hang out with their friends. It was Teddy, Cubby and I who were trapped in the neighborhood. Having the pool installed brightened our lives, but unfortunately, some of the neighbors tried to interfere with the pleasure it would bring us.

The couple next door to us filed a lawsuit against us over the ceiling fan. They wanted to prevent the ceiling fan from ventilating the room that housed the indoor/in-ground pool.

Though there was so much fuss about the fan, my brothers and I continued to play in the pool. My parents knew that the pool water was clean. It was no danger to us. As a result, all of my brothers and our best friend (or should I say only friend) enjoyed having the pool.

The ventilation of the room was required by code. At the demand of our neighbors, my parents attempted to run the swimming pool without the proper ventilation. The lack of this ventilation resulted in a buildup of chlorine gas that irritated the family's lungs and throats. It also resulted in an accumulation of moisture that resulted in a buildup of mold and mildew. My mom and dad were not about to allow these problems to occur, and worsen our health and fun. They fought the lawsuit with all their might in the case George Cook, et al. V. Charles J. DePrince, et al.

When the local newspaper telephoned us about writing an article on the fan case, my parents cooperated. A reporter wrote the article, which ridiculed the lawsuit, calling it, "The Fan that Roared."

This headline made us laugh. Why such a funny headline? The lawsuit began with the family whose house was located hundreds of feet away from our house. At first, these neighbors had filed a noise complaint, claiming that the fan, which was eventually surrounded by a cupola, roared so loudly that it caused their entire house to vibrate. An inspector was sent out to the Cooks' home, and his tests proved that they were unable to hear the sound of the fan from beyond our family's property line. They were also unable to feel a vibration.

Despite this finding, the Cooks invited several other neighbors to join their lawsuit. Some of these neighbors were from as far away as four houses down. They were also on the opposite side of the street. In order to include them in the lawsuit, the Cook's lawyer needed to convert it from a noise lawsuit affecting one neighbor, to a public nuisance lawsuit affecting several neighbors.

There seemed to be no way of escaping the lawsuit – until the plaintiffs became too angry in court, and shot themselves in the foot. This happened when one of the neighbors testified. He allowed his anger to erupt full force. In his self-righteousness, and certainty that the rest of the world believed as he did, the neighbor revealed to the Court that the suit had nothing to do with noise or vibrating bathrooms. It had to do with AIDS. That plaintiff told the Court that AIDS was being emitted into the air of the neighborhood through our ceiling fan.

The judge immediately ordered a recess, saying that he would return in an hour with his decision on the case. Even after the Judge stomped out of the courtroom in obvious anger, our neighbors were certain that they would win. They were astounded when the Court decided in favor of my family.

My family won the lawsuit, but by the time this happened, my youngest brother, Cubby, had died of AIDS.

My family was in deep mourning at that time. I missed
Cubby terribly. He had been my constant companion, and I
realized that I would soon face the same fate as my youngest
brother.

Chapter 13

When the pool was first built, I used to really swim. Swimming was something I could do very well despite the problems from my accident. My brothers used to love watching me do acrobatics in the pool. I used to hang upside down from the pool ladder with my head dangling in the water. I used to turn somersaults in the pool.

My favorite times playing in the pool were when Adam and Erik would let us sit on their shoulders, and play chicken. As time went on, Cubby and I grew too weak to swim or play chicken. Only Teddy still had strength and energy. By then, Mom would put me in an inner tube. She would swim back and forth pushing me along as she did laps, pretending to be a shark or dolphin.

In those days, while Adam and Erik were in college, and Teddy was still in middle school, Cubby and I spent every day at home. I was often content just to sit by Cubby's side while he slept. When he was awake, Cubby was my voice. He claimed to know what I wanted just by looking at me. Mom and Dad thought that Cubby claimed to know what I want based on what he himself wanted. One afternoon, however, I looked over at Cubby, and he said to Mom, "Mike is hungry. He would like a grilled-cheese sandwich."

Mom had seen no sign of communication between Cubby and me, so she said to him, "What do you want to eat, Cubby?" he answered, "A slice of peanut butter toast and jelly." He knew…just absolutely knew, as if by telepathy, that I wanted the grilled cheese, rather than the peanut butter and jelly.

In those last days of our time together, Cubby and I often sat at the computer and talked about two things that worried us the most. We were concerned about the homeless people who slept on the cold, snowy streets of Philadelphia, and the starving children of torrid, war-torn Africa.

We were a family of mixed religions. My brothers and I had decided to choose a religion that suited our blended family. We chose the Religious Society of Friends (Quakers). We belonged to a Monthly Meeting of Friends. It was a small meeting of elderly members, as such it was eager to have children as members. As a result, they were eager to support our efforts to feed the homeless on the streets of Philadelphia.

At that time, the homeless shelters in Philadelphia were closed on Sundays. It made us sad that these homeless families would not have a morsel to eat on that day. So our small meetinghouse of men, women and children would make sandwiches, bake cookies, and prepare hot beverages for the hungry.

My mom and dad had an old large 12-passenger van, which they had passed down to Adam. In it we piled food, warm drinks, blankets and clothing. Early on Sunday mornings, we would bring the sandwiches to the homeless. We learned that they loved the egg salad sandwiches best of all. The high fat in the mayonnaise and egg yolk, as well as the protein in the egg white, satisfied their hunger more than anything else. While my brothers and I were living with AIDS, it filled our hearts with joy to know that we could serve the needs of the poor and hungry of this earth.

In addition to helping the homeless, it was very important to me that Mom and Dad adopt children from war-torn Africa. Cubby, my youngest brother died of AIDS on a beautiful June morning in 1993. He was a brown-skinned boy, and reminded me of the children of Africa who were suffering in wars, or from African diseases like malaria, Ebola and malnutrition.

On a fall afternoon I wrote a message to my mother about adopting at least one African child. Mom had just finished infusing Teddy and me with one of our medical treatments for AIDS. It was called gamma globulin. It came in a large plastic bag with tubing, and it took hours to give us each a dose. When my mom read my message, she plopped down on the sofa, rolled her eyes, and looked like she wanted to collapse.

Teddy wrote me a message. It said, "Are you crazy, Mikey? Do you have any idea how hard our parents work to take care of us? Just what Mom and Dad need…more kids?"

It had never occurred to me that Mom and Dad might be overworked. I always thought that they enjoyed every minute they spent taking care of us. I was certain that if I kept pleading and begging, my parents might give in to my request.

After Cubby's death, I thought of the African children more than ever. I kept a notebook, and in it I wrote messages to Mom and Dad, over and over again, begging them to please adopt starving children from war-torn Africa. One day I even cut out one of these messages, and pasted it on the top of the television. I wanted my parents to see…one last message from me.

One of the problems of my having AIDS was that it weakened my immune system so severely that I contracted more than one illness because of it. The winter after Cubby died, I came down with two such diseases. One was toxoplasmosis, caused by a tiny parasite. It caused muscle pain, fever, and headaches, all of which lasted for many weeks.

The second disease that I came down with was cytomegalovirus encephalitis, better known as CMV. This was a virus that was usually only severe in infants and people like me with AIDS. It could cause seizures, which is what happened to me. I was sitting up in my bed watching Star Wars for about the millionth time. Suddenly, I suffered a seizure. I did not come out of it. The seizure lasted all day and most of the night. By the middle of the night, I had a fever of one hundred nine degrees. I died in my bedroom with my family surrounding me.

In those last moments, I prayed that my parents would find my messages about African children.

Epilogue

From Mike's Mom:

Four years had passed since we lost Cubby and Michael-Noah to AIDS. In that time, I worked on several non-profit causes. Members of the hemophilia community requested, on behalf of the U.S. Senate, that I write a book explaining the legal theory behind the transmission of HIV to the hemophilia population. Consequently, Random House published *CRY BLOODY MURDER: A TALE OF TAINTED BLOOD*, in 1997. It explained the basis for the tragedy of the transmission of HIV to ten thousand U.S. hemophiliacs. It established the legal theory for the American Hemophilia/HIV lawsuits. Among the lawyers who represented Hemophilia/HIV cases, the book became known as "The Bible of Hemophilia/HIV". It was a required reading for all of those lawyers, who handled Hemophilia/HIV cases.

After writing this book, I also advocated for changes in state legislation, which would open the statutes of limitation and enable hemophiliacs to successfully file their wrongful death and product liability lawsuits. I worked with other members of the hemophilia community for federal legislation that would compensate people with hemophilia for having contracted AIDS from a product approved by the

Food and Drug Administration. Most importantly, I worked to improve the safety of the nation's blood supply.

When all of that was said and done, I looked around at my empty nest and asked myself, "What should I do with the rest of my life?" Then I applied to law school.

At the age of fifty-one, I enrolled in law school at Rutgers University in Camden, hoping to reinvent myself. But despite this, I still felt like the mommy I had been for so many years. As that mommy, I had a gaping hole in my heart from the loss of my sons.

On a bitter cold January morning in 1999, I sat at my desk with a cup of steaming coffee within easy reach. I looked outside at the heavy snowfall. School had been cancelled that day, a rarity at Rutgers Law.

I decided to pour myself a second cup of coffee and read the newspaper, something I had not done since my first day of law school. Then I promised myself, that I would force myself to dive into the stacks of medical records and notebooks that surrounded me. I was facing a ten-day deposition for my sons' wrongful death lawsuits. Every other bereaved parent had faced only one or two days of deposition, but ten days were reserved for me because my book had created so many problems for the defendants, whose clotting factor had killed the boys with hemophilia. I knew to expect that they would grill me on every detail in the book. But my preparation would have to wait until ten o'clock, when I finished reading the newspaper. It would be my small act of defiance against the defendants.

Now suddenly on page six of the *Philadelphia Inquirer,* I noticed an Associated Press article about the civil war in Sierra Leone. It was a war that I hadn't heard of before, and

I was stunned to learn that while our newspapers had been silent, and our country had remained uninvolved, a war in Africa had been going on for nearly a decade. In this war, tens of thousands of people had been mutilated and killed. Thousands of children had been orphaned or abandoned.

The thought of the suffering children of Sierra Leone filled my heart with pain. When I finally turned to my deposition preparation, I found a message from my son, Michael-Noah. It had been stored in his notebook. My eyes filled with tears as I read, "Please adopt a starving child from a war-torn country in Africa."

Another message, which had been taped to the television, suddenly, as if by miracle, fluttered down. Memories of Michael-Noah came flooding over me. Deaf from birth, and because he was an excellent reader and speller, Michael-Noah preferred writing messages to using sign language. I found this particular message repeated throughout the notebook. I smiled through my tears as I remembered his earnest insistence. Burdened with the care of three terminally ill children, I had always answered, "No, we have enough kids."

Then I thought of the day in class when my Torts professor had stood at his podium and said, "Ah, compensation in the wrongful death of a child…that's a tough one. The settlements are generally low because no one is able to predict how a child might turn out. Would he grow up to be the person who discovers the cure for cancer, or become a serial killer? As a child, his value is only to his parents, and if they sue, it's not as if they'll get him back."

At that moment, my heart sank. I wasn't upset by the professor's comment about the low settlement. I didn't want to get rich on the pain and suffering of my children. As a matter of fact, I wanted to use it to help other children. But it was the last part of his sentence that bothered me, "…it's not as if they'll get him back." Deep down in a secret recess of my broken heart, I harbored a lingering fantasy that when the Court made its ruling for the plaintiffs, and the judge banged his gavel, my sons would enter the courtroom smiling as they ran into my arms. Now, I asked myself, "What would we do with our predicted low settlement, in the absence of our precious sons?"

I thought of the children of Sierra Leone. I knew that I certainly wouldn't have enough money to save all of the victims of that war. But perhaps there would be enough money to save one – a child in memory of Michael-Noah.

It would have thrilled Mikey to know that because of him, our family saved not one, but six little girls from the wars in Africa.